BEDROOMS

VITAE PUBLISHING, INC.
GRAND RAPIDS, MICHIGAN

First published in the United States of America by:
Vitae Publishing, Inc.
50 Monroe NW
Grand Rapids, MI 49503
Telephone: (616) 459-7600
Fax: (616) 459-9075

Other Distribution by:
Rockport Publishers, Inc.
146 Granite Street
Rockport, Massachusetts 01966-1299
Telephone: (508) 546-9590
Fax: (508) 546-7141

ISBN 1-56496-252-0

Front cover image: Credit on page 23
Back cover images: (clockwise from top left) Credit on page 29
                                            Credit on page 12
                                            Credit on page 8

Production by Sara Day Graphic Design

10 9 8 7 6 5 4 3 2 1

Manufactured in Hong Kong by Regent Publishing Services Limited

Introduction

There was a time, of course, when even ladies received genteel visitors in their boudoirs. That was when the boudoir was, perhaps, the only private place in a household shared with a variety of family and servants. But today, with so many rooms in most homes, the bedroom—especially the master bedroom—is truly a private place, usually reserved for those who sleep in it.

"Bedrooms mean different things to different people, even husbands and wives," says interior designer Ron Frey. "The husband may just want a comfortable place to sleep in, while the wife wants it to be romantic, the kind of space that wraps its arms around you, a type of escape from the world."

"To children, the bedroom is their special room, a room to be possessive about, and a place to express their own personality. For a teen, bedrooms are the places where secrets are told to friends—during 'sleeping-overs' or while talking on the phone—the place where an 'A' is achieved from studying hard, where things are memorized, where an instrument is mastered. Interior design needs to address all of these issues."

It is just these qualities that makes bedrooms difficult to plan, since creating a successful design involves intimate details. Designers often must ask questions such as, "What drawer do you keep your underwear in?" or, "What do you want to see before falling asleep—TV? Each other?"

Designer Janet Schirn has noticed that by the time she is finished fact-finding, she has often altered the way her clients see themselves. "I make them count everything they have; they find out they have forty-six ski sweaters and eighty-six pairs of shoes. Sometimes they are so surprised that they want to change the way they live. In truth, the environment with which we surround ourselves is important in shaping us, and in creating emotional and intellectual responses."

Modern bedrooms, more often than not serve several purposes: they are what designer Bettye Young calls the heart of the house. The bedrooms of today are places where clients make breakfast, watch TV, read, study, or do work with computers. Most are electronic nerve-centers, too, requiring a lot of modern equipment. "TVs, VCRs, phones, and remotes for everything. These things should not be intrusive, but should be easy to operate," says Young. (Her preference is to relegate them to a sitting area adjacent to the bedroom, on the principal that the most luxurious space is en suite.) To that group of modern gadgetry, designer Ron Frey would add the popular "client pleasers" of fireplaces, specialized lighting design, desks, armoires, and compact work centers.

Personal taste also plays a big role in bedroom decor, says Frey. He feels that it is the designer's job to know enough of the client's personality to be able to gauge this delicate balance. In fact, as Bettye Young has found, men often prefer a prettier bedroom than one might anticipate. The bedroom seems well within the feminine domain!

The design imperatives of bedrooms can be daunting if you consider Ron Frey's admonition: if it is a room used proportionately less than the others, it needs to accomplish the same amount of design impact in a shorter amount of time.

Vivian Irvine
Interiors

VIVIAN IRVINE
251 PARK ROAD
BURLINGAME, CA 94010
(415) 344-2222

PHILOSOPHY:
To be an effective residential designer is to be a good listener. Clients' lifestyles and preferences give us the direction we need to design a project which is uniquely theirs.

Communication and honesty between designer and client are the vital elements to success. The atmosphere of trust cannot be overrated as this is more than a business - at its best, it gives pleasure to all parties involved.

With its countless problems, this is at once satisfying, frustrating, challenging, exhausting, exhilarating, rewarding and at times, even a joyful experience.

Photos, above: John Vaughan; below: Jay Graham; photo opposite: John Vaughan

IDA Interior Design Applications, Inc.

IDA S. GOLDSTEIN, ASID
16 MUNNINGS DRIVE
SUDBURY, MA 01776
(508) 443-3433
FAX (508) 443-5251

PHILOSOPHY:
Our efforts focus on creating interiors that best reflect the individual desires and needs of our clients. We spend time listening to our clients to obtain a better understanding of who they are.

Using proper space planning and architectural details as a base, we add light, color, form and accents to create beautiful and special homes.

Above: Warm colors and contrasting textures help create a restful retreat
Below: Individually crafted furnishings contribute unique style to this relaxing room.

T. L. Knisely Interiors

TERRY KNISELY
EUGENE MONTGOMERY III
1911 EAST MARKET STREET
YORK, PA 17402
(717) 757-2555
FAX (717) 751-0704

Above: Meredith Magazine
Decorator Showhouse 1993

Above: Meredith Magazine Decorator Showhouse 1993

Deutsch/Parker Design, Ltd.

LARRY N. DEUTSCH, ASID
WILLIAM F. PARKER, ASID
325 WEST HURON STREET, SUITE 500
CHICAGO, IL 60610
(312) 649-1244 FAX
(312) 649-9617

The key to success is commitment to a set of principles based on achieving the highest level of professionalism. We work closely with in-house architects in order to design for the client's lifestyle and interpret those lifestyle needs selectively through fine art and furnishings. We believe that positive client communications, creative solutions and good business practices result in elegant design.

Anne Tarasoff
Interiors

ANNE TARASOFF, ISID
25 ANDOVER ROAD
PORT WASHINGTON, NY 11050
(516) 944-8913
FAX (516) 944-7256

PHILOSOPHY:
My approach to design is based
on the integration of the client's
lifestyle with a visual harmony
embracing uncontrived comfort.
I love to create romantic rooms that
have an understated elegance. This
is achieved with imaginative use of
color, pattern and detail.

William Hodgins

WILLIAM HODGINS, INC.
232 CLARENDON STREET
BOSTON, MA 02116
(617) 262-9538
FAX (617) 267-0534

A large, handsome mid19th century bed made in the Caribbean, painted by Yorke Kennedy, lends scale and comfort to this bedroom. Books and flowers make this room a special retreat.

V3 Design

VIORICA BELCIC
50 WEST 96TH STREET
NEW YORK, NY 10025
(212) 222-2551
FAX (212) 222-2201

PHILOSOPHY:
Being careful never to compro-
mise my professionalism, my goal
is to carry out the wishes of my
clients while gently steering them
toward choices of quality and
taste.

T. L. Knisely Interiors

TERRY KNISELY
EUGENE MONTGOMERY III
1911 EAST MARKET STREET
YORK, PA 17402
(717) 757-2555 FAX (717) 751-0704

Howard Alan Zaltzman Interior Design, Ltd.

HOWARD A. ZALTZMAN, ISID
1240 SOMERSET AVENUE
DEERFIELD, IL 60015
(708) 948-5734

I endeavor to make the entire design process as easy and enjoyable for the client as possible. The finished product is more important, but getting to the end result should be a pleasurable experience for the client, and not a nightmare of unanswered phone calls and broken promises.

Antine Associates Inc.

ANTHONY ANTINE
1028 ARCADIAN WAY
PALISADE, NJ 07024
(201) 224-0315 FAX (201) 224-5963

John Robert Wiltgen Design, Inc.

JOHN ROBERT WILTGEN, ISID
300 WEST GRAND AVENUE
CHICAGO, IL 60610
(312) 744-1151

PHILOSOPHY
The integration of art, architecture and design is what makes our homes timeless.

Lois C. Esformes
Interior Design, Inc.

LOIS C. ESFORMES
101 S. ROBERTSON BLVD., #213
LOS ANGELES, CA 90048
(310) 278-2252 FAX (310) 278-2326

Clara Hayes Barrett
Designs

300 BOYLSTON STREET
BOSTON, MA 02116
(617) 749-5876 FAX (617) 426-6415

Below: Pastels suffuse this Back Bay bedroom with good cheer. Family treasures and a painted ceiling add to the warmth. The bed is adorned with an antique quilt and lace.

Rodger Dobbel
Interiors

RODGER F. DOBBEL
23 VISTA AVENUE
PIEDMONT, CA 94611
(510) 654-6723

It is through the magic created by the positive relationship between the client and the designer, plus the tools of light, color, texture and scale, that one can interpret creatively and have the sensitivity to reflect the lifestyle of the client. With the addition of quality workmanship, the attention to details and good business ethics, the end results can only be a relaxed elegance that reflects warmth, livability and luxury. Above all, the design project should be a pleasurable experience.

Blakeley Bazeley, Ltd.

JAMES BLAKELEY III
TRACY UTTERBACK-BLAKELEY
P.O. BOX 5173
BEVERLY HILLS, CA 90210
(213) 653-3548
FAX (213) 653-3550

Our design solutions focus on creating timeless environments that continue to evolve. Clients' needs and desires, preferences of color and style are incorporated into the creative process. Emphasis on architectural details, lighting, and space planning lends itself to encompassing an eclectic group of textures, antiques, furnishings, and client collections. The combination results in an original design conducive to comfortable living.

Photos, above: Christover Covey; below: Leland Lee; opposite: Martine Fine

Joyce Crawford,
Interior Designer

JOYCE CRAWFORD
PHOENIX, AZ
(602) 952-0080

I thrive on lovely things and am stimulated by the avantgarde...by close color palettes playing on texture and line...by wonderful architecture which requires from me understated simplicity...by architectural shortcomings that stretch my imagination into solutions which create a whole new excitement.

Linda L. Floyd, Inc.

LINDA FLOYD
2 HENRY ADAMS STREET, M 50
SAN FRANCISCO, CA 94103
(415) 621-6756

Achieving a timeless and aesthetic reflection of my clientsí individual personalities and lifestyles is the hallmark of my firmís success. Inspired by the 18th centuryís pride in workmanship, quality materials and uncompromising attention to detail, my work strikes a balance between classical European elegance and our American demand for comfort. My most successful projects have evolved from a close working relationship with the client, resulting in a welcoming space that has a respect for the surrounding architecture and a sense of permanence, continuity and style.

Photo above: Ron Starr

Jack L. Clark

JACK L. CLARK
202 FAIR OAKS
SAN FRANCISCO, CA 94110
(415) 282-2000

Design should interpret the taste, lifestyle and personality of the client and not that of the designer.

Vivian Irvine
Interiors

VIVIAN IRVINE
251 PARK ROAD
BURLINGAME, CA 94010
(415) 344-2222

To be an effective residential designer is to be a good listener. Clientsí lifestyles and preferences give us the direction we need to design a project which is uniquely theirs.

Communication and honesty between designer and client are the vital elements to success. The atmosphere of trust cannot be overrated as this is more than a business—at its best, it gives pleasure to all parties involved.

With its countless problems, this is at once satisfying, frustrating, challenging, exhausting, exhilarating, rewarding, and at times even a joyful experience.

Photos, above: John Vaughan; below: Jay Graham; photo opposite: John Vaughan

Muriel Hebert, Interiors

MURIEL HEBERT
117 SHERIDAN AVENUE
PIEDMONT, CA 94611
(415) 547-1294

Clara Hayes Barrett Designs

300 BOYLSTON STREET
BOSTON, MA 02116
(617) 749-5876

I believe in and work for rooms that express the taste of my client and are fit for the uses to which they will be put. Quality is always essential. Rooms say a great deal about their occupants. Our homes symbolize our hopes, desires and our sense of accomplishment.

Anthony Hail Studio

ANTHONY HAIL
1055 GREEN STREET
SAN FRANCISCO, CA 94133
(415) 928-3500

Although Mr. Hail tends to have clients who prefer traditional interiors, he has successfully completed many projects reflecting contemporary design as well. Mr. Hail strives for a variety of things when designing an interior: an intuitive fusion of quality, craftsmanship, architectural detail of the highest quality, antique furniture and paintings, and upholstery in which soft colors highlight the furnishings.

The late Michael Greer described Mr. Hail's talents very well, "Anthony Hail is the only designer in the tradition of Elsie de Wolfe. He uses natural fabrics, silks, cottons, mostly off white and beige colors; white flowers in profusion, and a mixture of mostly European antiques, reflecting an enormously eclectic taste, with an overly fastidious eye."

Peter Moore Associates, Inc.

PETER MOORE
308 EAST 84TH STREET
NEW YORK, NY 10028
(212) 861-5544

Sylvia Schulman, ISID

RONI GILDEN, ISID ASSOCIATE
203 LAKESIDE DRIVE SOUTH
LAWRENCE, NY 11559
(516) 239-0362 FAX (516) 239-3147

10082 SPYGLASS WAY
BOCA RATON, FL 33498
(407) 482-6144

Above: Plaid wool walls contrast with crisp white antique linens to set the mood in this sophisticated bedroom based on the Provence region of France. The Steinlein poster is an outstanding example of French antique poster art.
Below: This bedroom sitting area is enhanced with Portuguese fireplace tiles, needlepoint rug and trompe l'oeil shutters. The portrait over the original mantel adds a touch of whimsy.

Hazell and Piening
Associates

HEATHER HAZELL
PETER PIENING

We are committed to creating a comfortable, functional, stimulating and exciting ambiance reflecting our clientsí individuality and lifestyle. There is no standard "look", but rather a diversified one—tailored to our clients' needs and finished to perfection.

Charlotte Moss & Co.
Page 29

CHARLOTTE MOSS
1027 LEXINGTON AVENUE
NEW YORK, NY 10021
(212) 772-6244

PHILOSOPHY:
By emphasizing the basic elements of comfort and by balancing scale, color and detail, we create interiors that reflect the lifestyles of our clients. A strong collaborative relationship with our clients culminates in surroundings that are elegant, distinctive, personal and functional.

Douglas Associates, Inc.

MELINDA DOUGLAS
2525 E. EXPOSITION
DENVER, CO 80209
(303) 722-6977

Right: The lightest possible tint of pink, matched on the custom painted drop-lid desk, is carefully planned as background for the deeper leaf green and rose reds of this cheerful bedroom and sitting area.

Blair Design Associates

DEBRA BLAIR
315 WEST 78TH STREET
NEW YORK, NY 10024
(212) 595-0203

Below: Medium to light peach stripes are both cheerful and restful as a background for this robust leaf green and floral fabric.

Anne Weinberg Designs, Inc.

ANNE WEINBERG
982 CHESTNUT RUN
GATES MILLS, OH 44040

Below right: A tint of grey leaning toward lilac combines with cream and soft pink to create this serene retreat.

Anthony Antine

1028 ARCADIAN WAY
FORT LEE, NJ 07024
(201) 224-0315

Veils of white fabric, white walls and white trim are a dramatic stage for the stark black bed frame. The black fireplace marble and painted tables continue the rhythm of color.

T. Keller Donovan

24 EAST 64TH STREET
NEW YORK, NY 10021
(212) 759-4450

Above: A palette of sunlight yellow and soft tints of leaf green and cabbage rose pink lend variety and depth to this sitting room/bedroom.

Anne Weinberg Designs, Inc.

ANNE WEINBERG
982 CHESTNUT RUN
GATES MILLS, OH 44040

Right: A tint of yellow resembling French vanilla ice cream wraps this charming bedroom.

David Holcomb Interiors

2188 BOHLER ROAD NW
ATLANTA, GA 30327

This vignette, a closeup of an elegant bedroom, focuses on the complimentary deep pink stain on the walls combining with a soft tint of apple green as well as gold, blue and a touch of red for a lively yet traditional palette.

Katrina Blades/Michael's Antiques

KATRINA BLADES
1831 29TH AVENUE SOUTH
BIRMINGHAM, AL 35209
(205) 871-2716

Creating classically designed rooms specifically tailored to each client's individual needs, lifestyle and taste is my primary role as an interior designer.

A 19th century Aubusson Portiere used as a bed hanging is the creative element of this bedroom.

Diane Alpern Kovacs,
Interior Design, Inc.

DIANE ALPERN KOVACS
4 MAIN STREET
ROSLYN, NY 11576
(516) 625-0703 FAX (516) 625-8441

An antique pine headboard,
English chintzes and an heirloom
quilt highlight this sunny bedroom.

Barbara Orenstein Interiors, Ltd.

BARBARA ORENSTEIN
MICHAEL ORENSTEIN
40 EAST 88TH STREET
NEW YORK, NY 10028
(212) 534-2103

"I am every bit as hospitable as I look." This is the philosophy of the husband and wife design team, Barbara and Michael Orenstein. In each project, they create an atmosphere of warmth, comfort and "hominess." Sophisticated, understated elegance is their signature of the English style interiors they create.

They believe their clients should feel equally comfortable at home alone or when entertaining a large crowd of friends.

Barbara, a graduate of New York School of Interior Design, teamed up with her husband after he sold his highly successful curtain, drapery and bedspread manufacturing business. Together, they work hand-in-hand on all the details of every project. Their work includes residences in the Tri-State area, Palm Beach, as well as several sailing yachts.

Stebbins & Co.

CINDY STEBBINS
79 EAST PUTNAM AVENUE
GREENWICH, CT 06830
(203) 661-0066
FAX (203) 661-0881

PHILOSOPHY:
Stebbins & Co. strives to create
interiors that are timeless, elegant
and appropriate.

Allison Holland

A delicate tint of butterscotch
looks exactly right as a background for antique furnishings
and a rich yellow floral bedcover.
The white pillows and woodwork
add sparkle to a monochromatic
color scheme.

Creative Decorating

168 POLOKE PLACE
HONOLULU, HI 96813

Allison Holland

Pale azure blue combines harmoniously with a natural wood ceiling finished in honeytones.

John F. Saladino, Inc.

JOHN F. SALADINO
305 EAST 63RD STREET
NEW YORK, NY 10021
(212) 752 2440

Work has always had a classical air. "I like visual classical quotations"—an historical reference.

A minimalist, creating a synthesis of historical and "modern" decoration.

Punctuates spaces with antiques and contemporary pieces. As long as they are of good quality, they make good companions.

A forerunner in the use of newest lighting technology.

From Italy comes his love of subtle color (sorbet colors) and rich objects, and his understanding of uses of space. One of his strengths is his extremely coherent comprehension of what he is trying to express in terms of design and decoration.

Negative spaces are as important as what you put in. The most important thing may be what you leave out.

In the end, the effect of the room and its furnishings should be like a good marriage—mutual dialogue showing mutual respect.

Weixler, Peterson & Luzi

STEVEN ANTHONY WEIXLER
WALTER BAYARD PETERSON
MARCELLO LUZI, ASID
2031 LOCUST STREET
PHILADELPHIA, PA 19103
(215) 854-0391

Photo: Under festoon curtains of Clarence House silk taffeta, a pair of Portuguese Louis XV fauteuils surround a Regency writing table from Kentshire. Bouillotte lamp is from Kensington Place Antiques; antique silver from Niederkorn. On the mantel sit three pieces of delft from Bardith. Oil painting above and watercolors to the left are from Frank S. Schwarz & Son.

L. B. Black Interior Design

LOIS BLACK
1134 WEST FARWELL
CHICAGO, IL 60626
(312) 761-9029

I see interior design as a partnership: My client provides me a history of life experience, memories and feelings; I offer my client an appreciation of the architectural space, a sense of scale and a knowledge of resources which serve to expand the clientís horizons. Together we create a vision of what is possible and work together to produce an environment in which the client feels truly at home.

Clara Hayes Barrett Designs

300 BOYLSTON STREET
BOSTON, MA 02116
(617) 749-5876
FAX (617) 426-6415

A traditional grace pervades this
guest bedroom. Delicate tambour
canopies the bed, and roses
"bloom" on the headboard and
dust ruffle.

Carol R. Knott
Interior Design

CAROL R. KNOTT
430 GREEN BAY ROAD
KENILWORTH, IL 60043
(708) 256-6676

My responsibility is to interpret the client's wishes and desires. Through open communication, we first identify a concept of how they would like to live. I then strive to implement the design process in a professional manner. I know I have done my part when the client is thrilled with the end result and I feel personally rewarded.

Paula Berg Design Associates

PAULA BERG
7522 EAST MCDONALD DRIVE
SCOTTSDALE, AZ 85250
(602) 998-2344

Creating a comfortable, timeless environment which reflects the client's lifestyle; emphasizing quality detailing and unique finishes form the foundation of my approach to design. I enjoy utilizing artists and craftsmen, especially those from the Southwest, for original one-of-a-kind effects, as whimsy is often introduced for surprise! Texture, rich natural fibers and materials, and antique architectural details, provide an earthiness which is the substance behind my work.

Julie O'Brien Design Group

JULIE O'BRIEN
546 SOUTH MERIDIAN, SUITE 300 A
INDIANAPOLIS, IN 46225
(317) 266-0772
FAX (317) 236-9402

"A home is an expression of its owners; a reflection of their dreams and ideals. Our work, as our clientele, is varied while sharing integration of architecture, use of detail and artistic integrity to create exciting, personal interiors."

Right: Romantic atmosphere created by hand rubbing iridescent paints.

Below: Custom designed rug.

Marc Kenneth Interior Design, Inc.

MARC KENNETH
330 EAST 38TH STREET
SUITE 36E
NEW YORK, NY 10016
(212) 986-0909

MARC KENNETH
330 EAST 38TH STREET
SUITE 36E
NEW YORK, NY 10016
(212) 986-0909

Kerry Joyce Associates, Inc.

KERRY JOYCE ASSOCIATES, INC.
6114 SCENIC AVENUE
LOS ANGELES, CA 90068
(213) 461-7808
FAX (213) 461-3814

Below: The serenity of white showcases a tranquil grass garden.

Kerry Joyce's interiors are characterized by a love for detail and fine materials. Able to work in a broad range of styles, he deftly creates satisfying interiors that reflect the personalities and lifestyles of his clients. "I love good design as well as comfort and I take it as a challenge to create an interior that will satisfy both." He believes strongly in the integration of architecture and interior design—having an affinity for both. "I reject trend or fad. Creating a timeless, enduring interior is very important to me."

Marie Mansour

I believe in not removing myself from my client's own comfort level, but rather merging their taste with my expertise and bringing it a step up from their expectations. Whether it is a work environment, a home or a 170 foot long yacht, it should be livable and a place you love to walk into every day.

Hendrix/Allardyce

ILLYA HENDRIX
THOMAS ALLARDYCE
335 N. LA CIENEGA BLVD.
LOS ANGELES, CA 90048
(213) 654-2222

Photo: A pair of 18th Century Japanese landscapes frame this curtained bed. Japanese porcelains with French bronze doré mounts are used as lamps. Walls are upholstered in a diamond print of heavy cream coloration.

Joyce Stolberg Interiors, Inc.

JOYCE STOLBERG
2205 NE 207TH STREET
NORTH MIAMI BEACH, FL 33180
(305) 931-6010
FAX (305) 931-6040

Residentially, my relationship with each client is relaxed and informal. Some of my best friends are clients! I prefer to install the entire concept, focusing on aesthetics and longevity because the client will have a long term relationship with their environment.

On a commercial basis, I concentrate on the company's product, service or image, and then I try to balance that with the client's artistic sense.

Joan Knight Interiors

JOAN A. KNIGHT
26561 WEST TWELVE MILE ROAD
SOUTHFIELD, MI 48034
(810) 354-5365

Susan Lapelle Interiors

SUSAN B. LAPELLE
500 HUNTERS CROSSING DRIVE
ATLANTA, GA 30328
(404) 671-1272
FAX (404) 671-1272

The process of decorating a space, either residential or commercial, should be as positive as the end result. Timeless rooms are comfortable, practical, pretty and tasteful. The fun comes when there is a whimsical touch and the owner's personality peeks through. This ongoing process works best when it evolves as an honest collaboration between client and designer. As the room is used and the people using the space develop and grow, it should reflect that evolution. With good planning, based on realistic budgets and timing, it can be a most rewarding experience.

P.T.M. Interior Designs, Ltd.

CAROL MELTZER
51 EAST 82ND STREET
NEW YORK, NY 10028
(212) 737-5139

ABOVE: Gentleman's dressing area and bathroom with custom interior closets and details.

BELOW: A touch of Savannah, in a New York apartment. A young woman's bedroom.

Beverly Ellsley, Inc.

BEVERLY ELLSLEY
179 POST ROAD WEST
WESTPORT, CT 06880
(203) 227-1157

Beautiful rooms are beautiful even when empty—furniture is a useful accessory for living in them. Space planning and design detailing are what make the difference—we specialize in just that difference!

We do architectural design, interior design, building construction and build our own handcrafted cabinetry—all with our own in-house craftsmen. We are able to control every facet of our projects—making it much easier for our clients—they have only one firm to deal with. We pride ourselves on being problem solvers.

We work in all styles. Our aim is to bring out the best of your style, not to impose ours on you.

Dessins, Inc.

PENNY DRUE BAIRD
129 EAST 82ND STREET
NEW YORK, NY 10028
(212) 431-1380

Creating your environment should be a pleasure, not an ordeal. I prefer to structure my business in such a way that purchases are made in a short period of time. Rather than order from obvious sources, I call upon a battery of European craftsmen, such as Mike Milillo in NYC, for custom upholstery and draperies. In this way, I can control the quality, detail, and timing of a given order. Frequent trips abroad permit access to unusual bibelots or collectibles that would otherwise be missed. I delight in creating a sense of "home." My interiors reflect the lives of the people who live in them. While fantasy and whimsy play a role, they do not belie the expression of the clients' true selves.

Design Works, Inc.

DIANE GOTÉ, ASID
SANDRA ELLIOTT
392 MORRIS AVENUE
SUMMIT, NJ 07901
(908) 277-2522

In all our design commissions, we like to capture the spirit of the clientís personality. The finished interior, we believe, must be the client's.

To create this artful mix, we carefully blend the essence of the clientís needs and desires along with a flavor for the exotic, the fanciful and the practical. We base all of our work on a strong architecturally designed foundation.

Pavarini-Cole Interiors, Inc.

CHARLES E. PAVARINI, III
ELIZABETH B. COLE
WEST REDDING, CT
(203) 938-9454
NEW YORK, NY
(212) 749-2047

As a design team we utilize our individual backgrounds and respective strengths in design construction and theatrical experience. An aesthetic objective is established by viewing the interior in terms of space, light and architecture. Mutual appreciation of this objective is enhanced through the client's full involvement in the design process which, in turn, enables us to more creatively and effectively apply the principles of good design. These same principles apply in the use of illumination to highlight function as well as dramatize one's perception of space.

When both the practical and aesthetic needs of our clients are comfortably met, we consider interiors to be successful.

Piemonte Minore Designs

RICHARD PIEMONTE
7 WOODACRES ROAD
BROOKVILLE, NY 11545
(516) 626-2332
SAL MINORE

First and foremost, our design philosophy is to create an interior which is timeless and most of all, livable. The proper use of color, texture and lighting is our prime concern. Evident in our interiors is an ambiance of romance and sophistication giving way to an opulent, sensual and classical style. Our approach, whether traditional or contemporary, is to create a successful interior using these elements of design, which help to make for a comfortable yet dramatic interior.

Noel Jeffrey, Inc.

NOEL JEFFREY
215 EAST 58TH STREET
NEW YORK, NY 10022
(212) 935-7775

Design expertise and the highest quality workmanship are basic to my firm's success. Extensive training in the history of design has inspired me to work with a broad range of styles from modern to French period interiors. Above all, I strive to create comfortable, livable environments that have an eclectic nature.

Photo: The pure elegance of cream tones in a comfortable, livable environment with French period furnishings.

Billy W. Francis
Design-Decoration

964 THIRD AVENUE
11TH FLOOR
NEW YORK, NY 10155
(212) 980-4151

Anne Tarasoff
Interiors

ANNE TARASOFF
25 ANDOVER ROAD
PORT WASHINGTON, NY 11050
(516) 944-8913
FAX (516) 944-7256

Pat Stotler
Interiors, Inc.

110 CORAL CAY DRIVE
BALLENISLES
PALM BEACH GARDENS, FL 33418
(407) 627-0527

James Northcutt
Associates

717 NORTH LA CIENEGA BOULEVARD
LOS ANGELES, CA 90069
(310) 659-8595
FAX (310) 659-7120

James Northcutt
Associates

717 NORTH LA CIENEGA BOULEVARD
LOS ANGELES, CA 90069
(310) 659-8595
FAX (310) 659-7120

John Robert Wiltgen

JOHN ROBERT WILTGEN
300 WEST GRAND, #306
CHICAGO, IL 60611
(312) 744-1151

Spillis Candela & Partners

800 DOUGLAS ENTRANCE
CORAL GABLES, FL 33134
(305) 444-4691

Cheryl Rowley
Interior Design

BRIGHTON WAY
BEVERLY HILLS, CA 90210
(310) 859-9185

Al Evans, IDG., ISID

1001 SOUTH BAYSHORE DRIVE
SUITE 2902
MIAMI, FL 33131
(305) 596-4626/531-5310
FAX (305) 538-0613

Ben Jones

ATLANTA, GA 30329
LOS ANGELES, CA 90069

Sandra J. Bissell
Interiors

93 MAIN STREET
NORTH ANDOVER, MA 01810
(508) 475-2060

93 MAIN STREET
NORTH ANDOVER, MA 01810
(508) 475-2060

Index of Interior Designers

Index of Photographers